Audrey Hepburn

An Audrey Hepburn Biography

Katy Holborn

Copyright © 2017.

All rights reserved. No part of this publication may be reproduced, distributed, or transmitted in any form or by any means, including photocopying, recording, or other electronic or mechanical methods, without the prior written permission of the publisher, except in the case of brief quotations embodied in critical reviews and certain other noncommercial uses permitted by copyright law.

This book is intended for informational and entertainment purposes only. The publisher limits all liability arising from this work to the fullest extent of the law.

Table of Contents

Audrey Hepburn – The Fairest of Them All

Audrey Hepburn, the Icon

Life Before Hollywood

The Start of a Career

Hollywood's Golden Girl

Audrey in Love

The Perks and Perils of Being a 'Mr. Hepburn?'

Audrey as a Mother

Love at Last, Until the Last

Humanitarian Work

Audrey Hepburn's Legacy

Audrey Hepburn – The Fairest of Them All

Audrey Hepburn, the Icon

What makes an icon?

An icon is the definitive symbol of something relevant, captured in a representative image. It comes from the Greek *eikon* – a likeness. It is recognizable and distinct, and usually points to something sought or desired. It is an effort to condense an idea, so that one look is all it takes for something to almost immediately be grasped and understood.

An anonymous, ordinary man with a bag of groceries stands defiantly before tanks of the People's Liberation Army in Tiananmen

Square, China. Four soldiers struggle to raise a U.S. flag in Iwo Jima during World War II. African American athletes raise their black-gloved fists at the medal ceremony of the 1968 Summer Olympics. A handsome Marxist revolutionary looks on with burning eyes, his dark hair wavy beneath a signature, starred beret. A disheveled genius playfully sticks out his tongue for a photo. In entertainment, a blond bombshell stands above the subway grates of New York City, and her flowing white skirt flies up with the wind – a strong case for why gentlemen should prefer blondes.

The latter, Marilyn Monroe, is as distinct and unforgettable a Hollywood icon as they come. She is perhaps, *The* Hollywood Icon. But her foil, a tall, slim, gamine ingénue, had her own mark to make in Tinsel Town – for who could forget the waifish Audrey Hepburn in a trim, black Givenchy dress, covered to the elbows in gloves, and thick ropes of pearls adorning her long, slim neck? This is Hepburn at her chic, most memorable best, in character as Holly Golightly, the charming but troubled New York socialite from the film, *Breakfast at Tiffany's* (1961).

It is unjust but irresistible to pit these two women together. Indeed, if later revelations hold true, Audrey Hepburn's most iconic role and unforgettable image might have actually been meant for Marilyn Monroe herself. Writer Truman Capote, on whose story the movie was based, had known the blond bombshell and is said to have wanted Monroe for the role of Holly. Monroe and Golightly, after all, had much more in common – Holly Golightly the character is the reinvention of a Texan vagrant named Lulamae Barnes, not at all unlike Marilyn Monroe's real past as Norma Jeane Baker. But for better or worse (for we will now never know), the role was won by Audrey Hepburn and she had owned it so completely that we can no longer imagine anyone else inhabiting that compelling character as if it were a second skin. Audrey Hepburn and Holly Golightly became intertwined, and cinema and ideals of beauty would never be the same again.

Marilyn Monroe and Audrey Hepburn's iconic, public images are easy to compare because they are almost polar opposites. There's the blonde in the flowing white dress with her playful, mature sexuality. On the other side, an almost childlike brunette restrained in chic, tailored black. Both women are breathtakingly, unforgettably beautiful in each of their own ways and any woman in the world can aspire to be either one of them. But history would show it is the sultry blonde who actually had an innocent, childlike vulnerability, while the slender brunette was the one with the steely strength. She was, after all, among many other things, a fundraiser and courier for the Dutch resistance during World War II – and she was only in her early teens at the time!

Audrey Hepburn died more than twenty years ago, of cancer in 1993. But her doe eyes continue to stare at us and seemingly look through us across time and space, immortalized and beloved by film. The camera, moving or otherwise, loved her and the light always found her, even from beneath the wide brims of her stiff, chic hats.

Her appeal cuts across genders and across generations. Her sense of style is immortal; at the very least, she helped place a little black dress in every girl's closet. She still sends women of all ages into Tiffany's in New York City, each one hoping to invoke her effortless, timeless, aristocratic style. Even women who have never seen any of her movies would be able to recognize the gamine woman in the pearls and the black dress. Even women who do not know her name could find in her an aspiration. An ideal.

She is a beacon of enviable style, sure, but clothing is just one part of her iconography. It must be remembered that in *Breakfast at Tiffany's*, she is as captivating in an LBD as she is in a man's white tuxedo shirt and an ostentatious eye mask. She simply had that mysterious X-factor, an irresistible inner light. She had carriage and grace. She had charm and easy humor. She had intelligence and warmth.

These are just a few of the things that makes a star like Audrey Hepburn transcend the movies to icon-status. She wasn't just beautiful; so many women, especially in her field, are beautiful. More than that, she became the symbol for an ideal of timeless relevance - that is, what it means to be a woman of style and substance. It was beyond beauty. It was a way of life and being.

Life Before Hollywood

Audrey Hepburn's most memorable works were about the power of transformation.

In *Breakfast at Tiffany's*, she sparkled as Holly Golightly, the scheming, charming, glamorous incarnation of an ambitious woman who would have otherwise simply been an ordinary little Lulamae Barnes with a quiet life in Texas. As Jo Stockton in *Funny Face* (1957), she is an intellectual snob, a hipster even before hipsters were a thing, turning from bookish to stylish thanks to a fashion editor with guts and a vision, and a photographer who steals her heart. In *Sabrina* (1954), she is the titular character, Sabrina Fairchild, caught between the affections of the two Larrabee brothers. The chauffeur's once-naive daughter, long ignored, deftly secures the affections of both men after a Paris makeover. In *Roman Holiday* (1953), for which Hepburn won a coveted Academy Award, she flips the script and goes from Princess Ann to commoner in disguise (still gorgeous and genteel, however), changing her hair and stealing away for a day of normalcy, freedom and romance. In *My Fair Lady* (1964), she goes for the full *Pygmalion* treatment as Eliza Doolittle, spunky, flower seller with a Cockney accent, subject to a bet that turns her into a lady of upper-class speech and fine manners.

She shone in these roles probably because she had a gift for transformation in real life. In her work as an entertainer, she shifted from stage actress to screen star and she would collect accolades wherever she went, as if it were so easy. Few in her field could match her Emmy, Grammy, Oscar and Tony wins. But beyond the entertainment industry, she would also wear many hats. She was a child working for the Dutch resistance during World War II, and had likely honed some of her acting skills there, in concealing not only her British citizenship and rearing, but also her dangerous secrets. She was a dancer and chorus girl before she made the graceful leap to acting on Broadway and in Hollywood. Near the end of her life, she would hang up the acting cap and take on the cause of children in landmark philanthropic work for UNICEF, which would eventually inspire more of her fellow entertainers to use their fame and influence for the greater good. She was a global citizen before it was cool.

Throughout all these changes, she was a woman always in motion but poised and held together by a calm sense of self, like the eye of a storm.

Edda Kathleen van Heemstra Hepburn-Ruston - Audrey Hepburn as she would eventually be known - was born a British citizen on the 4th of May, 1929, in Brussels, Belgium. Her father, Joseph Anthony Ruston, was born of privilege in Bohemia (a region later absorbed into the current Czech Republic) to an English father and a German mother. Like many aristocrats of his time, Joseph went to private school, spoke several languages and was a gifted horseman. He worked for the British diplomatic service, at which capacity he spent time on assignment in the Dutch East Indies. He found his first love there, but would eventually divorce her to marry a Dutch baroness, Ella van Heemstra. Van Heemstra, whom Ruston wed in 1926, was Audrey Hepburn's mother. Joseph and Ella moved to Brussels when he was working for a merchant company expanding operations out from London. Audrey was thus a British citizen born in Belgium. The family – Joseph, Ella, Audrey and two sons from the baroness' previous marriage, Alexander and Jan - would settle there.

The years between the end of World War I in 1918 and the start of World War II in 1939, was a time of rapid change in Europe. In Italy and Germany, Fascism – a political ideology characterized by intense nationalism, obedience to an all-powerful state, and focus on the needs of the community over that of the individual – was on the rise. In these interwar years, this particular brand of politics also entailed the buildup of military strength, the subjugation of groups or races deemed inferior, and the expansion of territory or reclamation of old (sometimes even mythic) territory, to promote or restore national grandeur and pride.

Ambitious, intelligent and charismatic men knew how to craft and deliver messages that would resonate with a dissatisfied people. Propaganda was paramount, and would bring popular support behind authoritarian leaders like Italian dictator Benito Musolini and the German fuhrer, Adolf Hitler. By May of 1939, Mussolini and Hitler would be formally allied in their shared objectives via the "Pact of Steel." Just a few months after that, in September, the German invasion of Allied country, Poland, prompted Britain and France to declare war on Germany. It was the start of the Second World War, though the events leading up to it, including the conclusion of the First World War and the infamously harsh measures imposed upon Germany for reparations as a result of it, have been in motion for years.

This is the scenario in which the young family found themselves. In its popularity, fascism could even manage to capture the support of Audrey Hepburn's mother and father, and in effect, link them with the Nazis.

When Audrey Hepburn's Hollywood star rose after World War II, her handlers and industry spin doctors found good cause to lionize her war efforts – but they had just as many incentives to closet away the family's links to the movement championed by the Axis powers. This means that some information are unconfirmed or inconsistent across sources, and are publicly revealed late, if they are ever revealed at all. Accounts vary, but reports would later come out that one or both of Audrey Hepburn's parents have participated in fundraisers for British fascism, and Joseph in particular may have been prominent enough within the movement to have shared a meal with Adolf Hitler in Munich along with a British fascist figure that he supported. Reports state he would even be sent to prison for a time, for his involvement in fascist activities.

But before that, for unknown reasons, Joseph left Ella and the family when Audrey was only six years old in 1935. Divorce came later when she was nine. It may have been because he tired of Ella's strong will. It may have also been because they differed in opinions and argued frequently, especially with Ella reportedly being more and more discomfited by Hitler's rise to power.

Whatever the reason for the family's breaking, Joseph lived in London where he added "Hepburn" to his name. The surname came from his mother's side and carried some prestige, but he may have also included it to seem more British as the lines in Europe began to be drawn leading up to the war. He wasn't quite in his immediate family's life at this time, but he was able to see Audrey occasionally there, as she attended a boarding school in Kent.

Joseph, like his ex-wife Ella, wasn't a particularly affectionate parent, but Audrey was a devoted daughter and open about her adoration for her father. She had actually advocated to continue to see him. By some accounts, he also showed continuing care for her welfare when, at the start of the Second World War, he reportedly bore his daughter away from Britain and brought her to her mother in the Netherlands, which was a neutral country. Other reports, however, say it was Audrey's mother Ella who had moved her back, hoping Holland's neutrality would spare the family from the ravages of war. Either way, at the outbreak of World War II,

Audrey was settled in Arnhem in Holland, in the false hope that it would be safer. The move started well enough, with Audrey able to pursue her education and study ballet.

While at school in London, she was shy and on the chubby side, making her the target of teasing in school. In Holland's Conservatory of Music and Dance, however, she enrolled, studied dance, and began to bloom. But Holland wouldn't be an untouched refuge for very long.

Despite the Netherlands' neutral standing, it was occupied by Nazi Germany in 1940. Audrey continued with her training in the arts, but few things stayed the same. Food was rationed and even then, there was little guarantee of getting anything. Fuel and heating were scarce too, but these were nothing compared to the images of violence she as a child caught in the war, would be subject to. There were men shot and killed on the streets. There was constant fear and uncertainty. As they did in other countries, Hitler's soldiers targeted Jews here too, and even got their tentacles into a few members of the Van Heemstra family, who had some Jewish ancestry.

In occupied Holland, Ella and her children did what they could to defy their occupiers and survive the war. Audrey's mother tried to pass as pro-German, but much of their valuables and properties would still be taken from them. One of her older brothers would be rounded up for a grueling labor camp; the other would go underground to avoid the same fate.

Audrey had her own part to play, too. Make that several parts to play. She was barely in her teens but she put her talents to good use, dancing in so-called "blackout performances." These were quiet shows behind closed doors and shuttered windows to no applause, so that they would not be discovered by the Germans as they raised funds for the Dutch Resistance and hid the money in their ballet shoes. She helped spread literature against the Nazis, became a child courier for the Resistance, and was reportedly in contact with downed Allied pilots secreted in Dutch homes, serving as messenger and delivering food. She also snuck in a few secret dance lessons for younger students, so that she could earn extra money for her family.

As the war raged on and the Germans crawled to a defeat, food became even scarcer. The diet comprised of diluted soup, improvised bread and sometimes even grass. Audrey suffered malnutrition and even had to stop dancing for a time. She shrank to less than 90 lbs., and had spells of other diseases. She would carry the effects of that difficult time in her body for ever afterwards – because that distinct waif attractiveness she would be known for had been carved by changes in her metabolism.

Thankfully, Audrey Hepburn would survive everything the Second World War threw at her, and so would her family. Even her half-brothers, including the one sent away to a labor camp, would find their way home a few weeks after the arrival of the Allied troops and the defeat of the Nazis in 1945.

The Start of a Career

During the war, Audrey Hepburn's love of the arts and performing helped carry her through tough times. It wasn't just that it helped her raise funds for her family and the Dutch resistance, it was also expression, and the normalcy of training while the world seemed to be falling all around her. After the war, she and her mother looked at dance in a different way – it wasn't just a means of surviving the present. It was also the path to the future.

Ella brought Audrey to Amsterdam, in the sphere of Dutch ballet legend Sonia Gaskell. Payment for the rigorous training would have been hard to come by, if Gaskell reportedly hadn't decided to give Audrey a chance to learn. By 1946, she was dancing at the Hortus Theater under the eagle-eye of critics. A couple of years later, she made her way to London to study at the prestigious Marie Rambert Ballet School. Funds were still tight, and for a time she had to put off enrollment. But eventually, between Audrey and her mother, they found ways to make it work. Ella was employed in a miscellany of jobs, including managing flats. Audrey did modeling work, and was again helped along by her teacher. Rambert even took her in for a few months.

Her ballet teachers must have seen some potential in her, but Audrey was also realistic about her prospects. She recognized her own limitations, and started to divert her ambitions to other forms of performing. She joined the chorus line of *High Button Shoes* for almost 300 performances. In 1949, she would be part of musical revue *Sauce Tartare* for hundreds of shows too, and *Sauce Piquante* after it. She also managed to land small parts in film and television, including *Young Wives' Tale* (1951) and *The Lavender Hill Mob* (1951).

The hardworking performer went from role to role, and eventually one part led to another, as if each one was a section of pavement winding its way to Hollywood.

In 1951, while in production for *The Secret People*, she secured a spot in *Nous Irons A Monte Carlo*. The shoot for the latter brought her to film in the French Riviera, which in turn brought her into the path of French writer Colette – who fancied she may have found in Audrey Hepburn, the titular character, *Gigi* for its adaptation as a play on

Broadway. That same year, Audrey would blow away William Wyler at a screen test and make her first step in conquering Hollywood. She was testing for *Roman Holiday* (1953).

Hollywood's Golden Girl

The kidnapping of Jaycee Lee Dugard in 1991 remains one of the highest profile kidnappings in history. In 1991, eleven-year-old Dugard was taken by Phillip and Nancy Garrido from the streets of her hometown in California. She spent eighteen years in captivity, during which time she was raped repeatedly and gave birth to two daughters, before being freed after Phillip and Nancy Garrido's arrest in 2009.

Audrey Hepburn was signed up for a Broadway play and a Hollywood movie. *Gigi* was a hit, and Audrey was considered a success in it. She struggled at the start, but improved through vocal coaching and hard work. She would continue to study and hone her craft even after *Gigi*'s success, at the Tarassova School of Ballet in Manhattan.

But her career wasn't the only thing going well for the gamine beauty. Audrey Hepburn in 1951 was successful and also in love.

Her first serious relationship had been a short-lived one with Marcel le Bon, when she and the French singer / lyricist were in *Sauce Piquante*. Le Bon was followed by multimillionaire James Hanson, who was an industrialist and whose family was in the trucking business. They started a relationship after production for *The Lavender Hill Mob* in 1949. When she did *Gigi* in 1951, it was fortunate that his work sometimes took him to New York (aside from Britain and Canada), and they managed to see a lot of each other during this period.

He would even put a diamond engagement ring on her finger in 1951. It must have been a heady time alongside all of her success, but by 1952, the demands of her rising career began to take a toll on their relationship. Immediately after *Gigi* – as in, on closing night! - she headed to Italy for the filming of *Roman Holiday*. The wedding with Hanson, planned for the Spring after *Gigi* but before her work began for *Roman Holiday*, was postponed. When her *Roman Holiday* filming ended, however, she plunged right into a road tour for *Gigi* in America, and there was yet another wedding postponement. Eventually, she and Hanson split. She wanted to give proper time for the man who would be her husband, which the demands of her job would not have been able to allow at that point of the career she had worked so hard to achieve.

Audrey Hepburn may have lost Hanson, but she gained the love of critics and audiences alike, when *Roman Holiday* came out in 1953. She wasn't just a fresh-faced beauty, another one of Hollywood's fine young things of the moment. She also had 'It.' She knew how to carry clothes and the fashion industry was also starting to pay attention.

It certainly helped that she was also a force to be reckoned with in acting. As a matter of fact, her star-making turn in *Roman Holiday* – her first major role, really, would help her nab an Academy Award for best actress in March of 1954.

Her *Roman Holiday* triumph was just the beginning for Hollywood's delightful ingénue. By 1953 she was filming *Sabrina* in Long Island, New York with William Holden and Humphrey Bogart as the wealthy Larrabee brothers vying for the affections of the chauffeur's fetching daughter, under the direction of Billy Wilder. If *Roman Holiday* helped Hepburn catch the attention of eagle-eyed fashion aficionados everywhere, *Sabrina* was where she would make a bold and conscious, indelible mark on the industry.

Paramount's famous wardrobe supervisor, Edith Head, was responsible for Audrey Hepburn's stunning turn as Princess Ann in *Roman Holiday*. In *Sabrina*, however, the wardrobe supervisor's services would only be used for a few ensembles in the film, and not particularly significant ones at that. Such a job would instead fall upon the shoulders of a young French design sensation named Hubert de Givenchy, who was only 26 years old at the time. The idea of using genuine French couture purchased in Paris for use in the movie was reportedly Hepburn's. She was a lover of fashion, and had once described it as so much of a passion that it was *"practically a vice."*

Givenchy and Hepburn were brought together by Gladys de Segonzac of Schiaparelli, and wife of the head of Paramount in Paris. At the time, *Roman Holiday* wasn't released yet and Givenchy wouldn't have known much (if anything at all) about the persuasive waif knocking on his door and seeking his services. But she explained her purpose to the hot young couturier of the moment, and though he was hesitant due to workloads for an upcoming collection, he let the winsome ingénue try on a few sample clothes that he had in his atelier. They were from the previous season, but the ecstatic Hepburn all but transformed before their very eyes in Givenchy's fashions. Givenchy would later describe Audrey as having the ability to give life to clothes. They became fast friends and would work together not only for seven more movie projects, but he would also dress her in her personal life. They were both disciplined and hard-working and certainly did a lot of business together, but they were more like brother and sister. He was her beloved confidant, privy to the most intimate parts of her life, including details of her romantic entanglements and later, even her will.

Billy Wilder approved of Hepburn's choices for *Sabrina*, but as filming progressed, became all the more rapturous of his lead actress' radiance in signature Givenchy. Scenes of the movie seemed to weave outwards from how Hepburn looked, affecting how they were shot and edited, and even affecting how some of the encounters between characters were re-written. Audrey was simply captivating, and would even ensnare the real-life affections of her co-star, the married and 11-years older, William Holden (the affair wouldn't get very far, but more on the loves of Audrey Hepburn, later).

In *Sabrina*, Hepburn showed that she knew what she wanted for a role. She knew what she wanted in a designer. She had an understanding not only of her own preferences, but also what looked good on her. She was detail-oriented and wasn't afraid of infusing a look with quirk and character. She was only in her 20's and a Hollywood newbie, but she already had a distinctive sense of style. That style flowed from and into her and her character fluidly, such that sometimes, it was hard to tell where off-screen Audrey Hepburn started and where the on-screen character began.

When the film opened in the United States in 1954, it was well received. But Audrey, in particular, was described ecstatically. Critics called her magical, beguiling, bewitching – as if she were a rare, otherworldly creature of legend and fairy tale which, in a way, she was.

Sabrina fever – or perhaps, Audrey fever? – wasn't just sweeping across America. Premieres and live appearances by the star sent the fan frenzy across the seas, too. In the Netherlands, where the premiere was also a homecoming for Audrey in late 1954, there were modeling shows for Givenchy and signing events which helped raise funds for Dutch veterans. In France in early 1955, promotions around the premiere were focused on the film's links to French fashion.

While *Sabrina* was a big commercial and critical success and she seemed confident, however, Audrey Hepburn could be very critical of her own work. She had once been horrified at the kind of salary her acting performances could command, a salary that would eventually catapult her into being among the highest-paid actors in the globe.

She was uncomfortable with it and felt unworthy. Her acting insecurities was also probably why she paid so much attention to wardrobe, aside from her sheer love of fashion; she used her character's clothes to tell a story, allowing her to flesh out a role and help improve her dramatic technique.

Why she should have been worried so much about her acting prowess is a mystery. Her performance in *Sabrina* got her another Academy Award nomination in 1955, though she would lose this race to Grace Kelly's *A Country Girl*. If she had any more reservations after that, one would think that the other critical successes of her career would be some balm to her acting insecurities. Over the course of her career in film, television and stage, she would garner multiple nominations and wins from various prestigious bodies. The Academy Awards would nominate her as Best Actress in a Leading Role for *The Nun's Story* (1959), *Breakfast at Tiffany's* (1961) and *Wait Until Dark*, (1967). The Golden Globes would honor her too, with a Best Actress-Drama win for *Roman Holiday* (1953), and nominations for her acting work in the same films as that mentioned in the Academy Awards list above, plus for her work in *War and Peace* (1956), *Love in the Afternoon*, (1957), *Charade* (1963), *My Fair Lady* (1964), and *Two for the Road* (1967). Various projects would also gather recognition from the Primetime Emmy Awards, the BAFTAs, the Screen Actors Guild Awards, the Grammy's, and the New York Film Critics Circle.

Outside of film and television, Audrey Hepburn would also find recognition for her work on the stage. In 1954, she starred in *Ondine* on Broadway, and walked away with a Best Stage Actress Tony award for her efforts. She was starring opposite one Mr. Mel Ferrer, at the time.

Audrey in Love

Audrey Hepburn was a lovely woman with so much to offer. Beauty, intelligence, discipline, manners, talent, affection... the list could go on and on. She was forgiving and admiring of her father, even after Joseph left the family. Hubert de Givenchy had fond memories of getting simple phone calls where the superstar would just express her love of the man who helped forge her style and whom she considered a brother. She was a good daughter, who helped provide for her family during the war, and would continue to offer them support when she found success as an actress. Even her estranged and eventually remarried father, who settled quietly in Dublin, Ireland later in life, would get both correspondence as well as financial support from Audrey. So how could she have been as a girlfriend and wife? What would it have been like, for a man to be lucky enough to have those signature doe-eyes looking at him, and only him, with such sparkling, cinematic love and longing?

At this point, we already know that Audrey reportedly had a short-lived romance with fellow stage performer, Marcel le Bon. He was soon followed by wealthy businessman James Hanson, with whom she split up amicably when it became clear that the demands of their careers seemed incompatible to keeping their love alive. They were so close to the altar that she already managed several wedding dress fittings with the sister designers, Fontana. The dress would (*of course!*) later be auctioned.

Eventually though, it would be one fairly controversial Mr. Mel Ferrer who would win the hand of the gamine superstar. They met at a party in London in 1953, around the time of the London premiere of *Roman Holiday*. Ferrer, an actor and director, wasn't quite the youth and stability of Audrey's previous love, James Hanson. At the time, Ferrer had been divorced twice, had several children, and was 12 years older than her. But they had chemistry, and sparks flew. Shortly after their fateful meeting, Ferrer sent her the script for a Broadway production of *Ondine*, and they both starred in the well-reviewed staging in February of 1954 after her work filming for *Sabrina* finished. Her time in *Ondine* would be cut short due to health problems, but what she showed on the stage was enough to secure her a Best Actress Tony award.

The show closed in July and Audrey worked on restoring her health, finding refuge in Switzerland. It was also where she and Mel married in September, 1954. They honeymooned in Italy where he was working, and in the Netherlands where she was promoting *Sabrina* and doing fundraisers for the League of Dutch Military War Invalids.

Audrey and Mel tried to make their marriage work. They did several projects together, and when their individual acting commitments took them to different locales, they hopped around from country to country just to see each other.

Hepburn and Ferrer were together in Italy for the filming of *War and Peace* (1956) and in Hollywood for *Green Mansions* (1958) and the television movie, *Mayerling* (1957). The projects were unfortunately poorly received, but the Ferrers never lacked for work and Audrey in particular had the pick of them; around this time, she would be doing *Funny Face* (1957) with Fred Astaire, as well as the high-grossing *The Nun's Story* (1959). Besides, the Ferrers had other concerns.

Audrey had a miscarriage in March, 1955. She suffered another such loss in 1959, shortly after a fall that broke her back while filming *The Unforgiven* (1960) in Mexico. When she got pregnant again, she resolved against taxing her body with the rigors of acting work until she gave birth. Her commitment to having a child had her turning down projects like *The West Side Story* and an Alfred Hitchcock film. Her next project would be after the birth of her and Mel's son, Sean, who was born in Lucerne, Switzerland in July, 1960.

After Sean's birth, she worked on a 'little' project called *Breakfast at Tiffany's* (1961), for which she would always be remembered and cherished by film and fashion fans everywhere. Few things could dim Audrey Hepburn's star after that – she shone even in small roles and flops. But one role would bring her criticism, that of the lead, Eliza Doolittle in *My Fair Lady*. The role was originated by a young and so wonderfully promising Julie Andrews on Broadway, but Andrews did not have the cachet yet in Hollywood for them to risk bringing her into the screens to play the part. The film had a big budget, and producers were not comfortable resting the film on a relative unknown's shoulders. Audrey Hepburn's efforts at a cockney accent would be panned, and though she did some singing, she was ultimately dubbed over by Marni Nixon. That year, the Academy Award did not bother with handing her a nomination. That year, the Best Actress Award went to Julie Andrews, as the titular role in *Mary Poppins*.

The Perks and Perils of Being a 'Mr. Hepburn?'

Being a mom barely slowed down the superstar's movie career, even though she prized her family above all else. Aside from *Breakfast at Tiffany's* and *My Fair Lady*, Audrey worked in other high-profile projects; with *Roman Holiday*'s William Wyler again, for *The Children's Hour*; with her *Sabrina* co-star William Holden in *Paris When It Sizzles*; and with *Roman Holiday* leading man, Cary Grant in the hit, *Charade*. Mel Ferrer kept busy too, but his wife was clearly the bigger star. Then again, who could've been bigger than Audrey Hepburn at her peak then, when her residual light *now* can still outshine many of today's artists?

Inevitably, because husband and wife were in the same field and the disparity in their careers had the woman doing much better than the man, people theorized that such a reversal in power dynamics can create strain in a marriage. He could be domineering and controlling to her too, some observers noted. While it couldn't have been easy being regarded as 'Mr. Hepburn' and Ferrer had to find ways to assert himself, however, he always did say he preferred being behind the scenes to acting and that it was unrealistic to compete with Hepburn, so perhaps it was a contributor to the failure of the marriage, but it wasn't the only one. Maybe it was actually because he wanted her to continue working in film, while she wanted to spend more time with family, as some reports suggest. At any rate, they always did have a complex love story so probably, the eventual end of their marriage was just as intricate, a mix of several factors rather than just a single cause.

Melchor Gaston Ferrer was born in Elborn, New Jersey in 1917, to a surgeon and a New York socialite. His posh background, along with his pricey private schooling and attendance at Princeton, gave him an aristocratic quality to match his dashing looks. He was cosmopolitan and multi-lingual. He didn't finish schooling in Princeton, but did leave with the Playwright's Award and ambitions of becoming an actor. He fought his way to his dreams, starting out as a chorus dancer on Broadway and eventually landing small roles in plays. He would also find work in radio and as a producer and as a director. He would straddle that line between being on screen and being away from it all throughout his professional life, as he got more and more successful. His time in Broadway and Hollywood would be true to that pattern, of acting in one project and directing or producing another. He also co-founded La Jolla Playhouse in California.

Indeed, over the course of his career, he would have over 100 film and television credits under his belt, for acting work and for work behind-the-scenes. His acting is best remembered for compelling roles in *Lili* (1953), where he played an embittered puppeteer pining for Leslie Caron's title role; and in swashbuckler classic *Scaramouche* (1952) as the ruthless swordsman, Marquis de Maynes. In this movie, Ferrer as de Maynes played the villain in one of cinema history's greatest swordfights. It is an even more stunning feat, considering Ferrer had conquered mobility problems in his arm after catching polio earlier in his career.

He would also be remembered for directing Audrey in the unfortunate *Green Mansions* (1959). It was a big flop in her otherwise stellar career. He should, however, also be remembered for steering Audrey toward her Tony Award-winning Broadway role in *Ondine* in 1954, and for the hit *Wait Until Dark* (1967), which he produced. Hepburn would get her fifth and final Best Actress Academy award nomination for her role in that film.

Mel Ferrer would find love with four women in five marriages over the course of his life. He married Frances Pilchard twice, with Barbara Tripp in between their two marriages. He had children with both women, and was still married when he met Audrey Hepburn at a party in 1953.

Ferrer and Hepburn had immediate chemistry, but chemistry alone does not make a lasting relationship. He was married, had children, was much older, and was not quite approved by Hepburn's mother, the baroness Ella van Heemstra. The relationship wouldn't go far and soon, Hepburn would be in the sphere of handsome, notorious Hollywood playboy, William Holden.

Holden and Hepburn were co-stars in *Sabrina*. They were filming in New York and became allies in a tense set, where pressure on the Hollywood newbie was high, on top of all of them having to contend with the brooding but gifted veteran, Humphrey

Bogart. Bogart was much older than Holden and Hepburn, and was reportedly skeptical of Holden's acting skills, felt threatened by Holden's rapport and work history with director Billy Wilder, and was uncomfortable in the romantic comedy genre, which was a departure from his usual fare. In this environment, Holden and Hepburn reportedly connected and fell passionately in love. Ardis, Holden's tolerant wife who let her notorious husband have a long romantic leash, met Audrey over dinner and knew she had a genuine rival who was not at all like Holden's previous, passing flings. After that meeting, she allegedly asked her husband to interact with Audrey only in a professional capacity, but he wouldn't have it. What would eventually end the affair, however, was that Audrey reportedly wanted to have children badly, while Holden, who had a vasectomy, could no longer provide. The relationship ended in heartbreak, especially for Holden who would resort to reckless behavior and drinking to such a self-destructive level that when he worked with Audrey again for *Paris When It Sizzles* in 1962, he looked more haggard and eventually had to go to rehab.

Not that Audrey Hepburn would have been free to pursue a love affair with Holden when they reunited to film *Paris When It Sizzles*. By that time, she was already long married to Mel Ferrer, who made a comeback in Audrey's life after her romance with Holden fell apart and Ferrer had acquired his third divorce in 1954. That year, they worked on the successful *Ondine* on

Broadway, and would marry shortly afterwards.

The marriage wouldn't last for very long. Their union would suffer the same fate as that of Ferrer's previous other walks down the aisle - divorce. Allegedly, aside from the strain the disparity in their careers may have contributed to the crumbling of their marriage, Ferrer was also somewhat neurotic and overprotective. He controlled interactions with his wife, secreted away her phone number, and was often her spokesman. The term "Svengali" would be mentioned a few times regarding Mel Ferrer's handling of Audrey Hepburn, after the fictional villain of the 1894 novel *Trilby* by George du Maurier. Svengali puts model Trilby under his spell, turning her into a star but manipulating her and keeping control of her.

These are accusations Hepburn would laughingly brush off, and some of Ferrer's defenders say it was also Hepburn's way to defer to her husband anyway. At any rate, it is inconclusive whether or not this dynamic contributed to the end of their marriage, for Audrey wouldn't say bad things about Mel Ferrer afterwards, nor would he do the same of her. It probably didn't help them though, that much of her and Ferrer's film work together, with the exception of *Wait Until Dark*, were not being received well by audiences and/or critics either.

Another factor that could have contributed to the dissolution of the marriage was that Mel Ferrer allegedly had girlfriends … Not that the revered Hepburn was completely saintly. If rumors are true, Hepburn may have also indulged in a few extramarital romances of her own, such as one with screenwriter Robert Anderson during the filming of *The Nun's Story* in 1957, or one with *Two for the Road* (1967) co-star Albert Finney. Ferrer and Hepburn began living separately in 1967, and announced their divorce in 1968 after 14 years of marriage and one son, Sean Hepburn-Ferrer. Sean went to Audrey's custody.

Mel Ferrer continued to work in various projects after the split, with fans able to spot him in American television shows like *Falcon Crest*, *Fantasy Island* and *Murder, She Wrote*, and a few other projects from nations as varied as France, Germany, Italy and Spain. He and Audrey would speak extremely sporadically after their marriage ended, with some reports saying they spoke as little as twice over 25 years. He was visibly shaken by her death, however, reportedly weeping openly in her funeral and needing comfort from the son they shared, Sean. Ferrer outlived Hepburn by many years, and passed away at age 90 in Santa Barbara, California in 2008. At the time of his death, he was married to Beligian, Elizabeth Soukhotine, whom he wedded in 1971.

Audrey as a Mother

The 1968 divorce between Ferrer and Hepburn was hard on the couple's son, Sean. It was already difficult being the only child of two stars; when they were busy jetting around the world for work, he would often end up with his grandmother and his nanny. But Mel and Audrey tried not to fight in front of him even at the height of their troubles, and they did whatever they could to assure Sean that he was loved and that the fracture of their family was through no fault of his. They also did not put him in the middle of their troubles, by refraining from saying anything bad about each other. Later, Audrey Hepburn would say that sometimes, the relationship between two good, loving people just doesn't survive a difficult situation even if you try and try.

Sean loved both of his parents. He would have fond remembrances of his mother being silly, and telling him stories or nursing him through illness. She would sometimes surprise Sean's visiting friends by her normalcy, wearing an apron and preparing a meal. Sean and Audrey were close, and after he was born she took on less acting work even if the parts and offers continued to come. Audrey always wanted children and a family, and she was clear on her priorities at that point of her life.

She went into semi-retirement, and found love anew in her second and final marriage, to Italian psychiatrist / neurologist Dr. Andrea Dotti in 1969 whom she met at a private cruise. She was prioritizing her family at this point, and had reportedly been wanting a quiet life being a doctor's wife. They settled in Rome with Sean, but she kept a home in Switzerland, managed by her mother who also resided there. The marriage between Dotti and Hepburn produced another son for Audrey, Luca Dotti, in 1970. At that point, she was 40 and was by all accounts a supermom, cooking meals and walking her children to school.

By many accounts, it was hard to drag her back into the movie business. She had reportedly asked not to be sent scripts as early as 1967. According to Terrance Young, with whom Audrey worked in the hit, *Wait Until Dark*, getting her into a project included an intricate wooing that involved getting her to even entertain the possibility of returning to film work; then getting her to actually read a script; then pitching her on how good it is; then convincing her being away for a few weeks wouldn't be detrimental to her kids; then talking about things like her cherished topic of costumes; and then, *then* one was still likely to get a 'no thank you.'

Few things would draw her out of the relatively quiet family life she had fashioned for herself. Among them, charity work with UNICEF, and the high-profile film, *Robin and Marian* with Sean Connery. Film reviews were mixed when they came out, but as always, Audrey Hepburn was welcomed back and cherished. She would also make a few public appearances in the mid-1970s, including presenting the Best Picture Oscar in 1975 – for which she, in a fairly minor role as presenter, was actually given a standing ovation.

Even when she placed such a priority on her family though, her marriage still wouldn't work out. The doctor she married had reportedly been cavorting around with other women. The marriage ended after 13 years, as more and more reports of Dotti's scandalous activities hit the press. The Dotti divorce wouldn't be until 1982 but Audrey would be rumored to have an extramarital fling prior to that, with *Bloodline* co-star Ben Gazzara in 1979. Gazzara was also said to be in an unhappy marriage, a point of commonality for the co-stars. Aside from that rumored relationship, when the split with Dotti came along, Audrey was already in another, this time with Dutch businessman and actor, Robert Wolders.

Love at Last, Until the Last

Married twice, divorced twice.

But never was Audrey Hepburn without love.

The man with whom Audrey Hepburn spent the rest of her life was actually someone whom she never married: Robert Wolders. He was born the 28th of September, 1936 in the Netherlands, and was a Dutch businessman and actor. He was very handsome, known for his work in the hit series *Laredo*, for which he did 26 episodes in the 1960s. He was famously the widower of British-American actress Merle Oberon, so in some ways, he was used to being with a woman in the spotlight.

The exotic Merle Oberon, Wolders' first wife, is known for her dramatic beauty, which ranked among the best of Hollywood's Golden Age, even if her filmography wasn't quite filled with hits. She is best remembered for her role as the heroine in William Wyler's adaptation of *Wuthering Heights* (1939), where she starred alongside Laurence Olivier. She is also remembered for her colorful personal life. Oberon was mixed-race, and grew up in India at a difficult time. She had a complex family history hidden beneath a convoluted origin story she passed off as fact on her way to stardom. Oberon met Wolders while making her final film, *Interval* (1973) – she played an aging beauty falling for a handsome young artist. The co-stars brought their roles from the reel to reality, as they fell in love and married in spite of a 25-year age gap. She passed away in late 1979. Her widower, Wolders, would thereafter become the love of another brunette beauty's life.

Hepburn and Wolders met at a party. He had asked her out to dinner, but she said she had a shooting schedule. Wolders would later say he thought he was being gently rebuffed, but afterwards, she would be the one to issue him an invitation. They had great chemistry almost immediately, and he would be her companion from 1980 to her death in 1993. They never took that walk down the aisle, but they always considered themselves unified as if in marriage.

Hepburn and Wolders were a mature couple who found each other relatively late in life but to them, the timing was perfect. They were in their 40's but still so beautiful, and many of their publicly available photographs would show them in gowns and tuxedos in the cosmopolitan set's hottest ticket events. A fashion gala here, a Hollywood event there, even one with Ronald Reagan at the Gipper's White House in 1981. But it wasn't just about glamour. He joined her all over the world in her charity work too, and they had private photos at home as well, with pets and no makeup, sitting on the couch, taking a walk… moments of quiet, romantic ordinariness. He was indeed very supportive of her, even as early as 1980, when he joined her in Dublin to see her ailing father before he died. Their time together included some of the most critical moments in her private life; the passing of her father, the passing of her mother in 1985, and the marriage (though short-lived) of her eldest child, Sean, in 1985. They were also together when she received her cancer diagnosis in 1992.

Audrey Hepburn's shocking diagnosis came 12 years after she and Robert Wolders started a life together. She was the epitome of grace right up to the very end. When she was told she had a few months left to live, she reportedly feared pain, but not death. One of her final wishes was to be in Switzerland for her last Christmas, and her loving friends moved heaven and earth to grant it. At the time, her health was already in a fragile, precarious state. A normal flight would have been her undoing, so a private jet was arranged for her by her dearest pals, Hubert de Givenchy and Bunny Mellon. Shortly after Christmas, she passed away in January, 1993.

Humanitarian Work

Audrey Hepburn was a lovely woman who was generous with her heart, not only for the men she loved, not only for her family and friends, not only for the people who delighted in working with her, but also for the struggling children of the world. In 1989, she was appointed Goodwill Ambassador for UNICEF – among the first and most prominent of the celebrities to share their time and talents with the organization.

UNICEF was founded in 1946, as The International Children's Emergency Fund ("ICEF"), following the unprecedented horrors faced by children in the wake of World War II. They worked to provide aid for children's health without discrimination, regardless of politics – a policy that would bring them to such places as Vietnam, Cambodia, Sudan and Iraq, even in times of conflict. Eventually, it became a permanent agency with the United Nations, and removed "International" as well as "Emergency" from their name as their work extended not only to post-war aid and helping nations, but also to activities like eradicating preventable childhood diseases, improving water access and sanitation, providing maternity care, instituting nutrition programs, livestock training and promoting childhood literacy and education, for needy countries as well as classes like the urban poor within nations. They retained the established acronym of "UNICEF," however.

Their first celebrity "Ambassador at Large" was American entertainer, Danny Kaye, who was appointed in 1954, and he would be followed by many A-list names willing to share in UNICEF's vision of improving children's lives, anywhere in the world that they may be. Some of the most famous, international names to hold the esteemed role are pop superstar Katy Perry, sporting legends Serena Williams and David Beckham, Jordan's Queen Rania, Hong Kong crossover megastar Jackie Chan and Oscar winner and Hollywood institution, Susan Sarandon.

Audrey Hepburn was one of their most prominent ambassadors, and few could match her right to speak on behalf of innocent children caught in hardship and/or conflict. She was barely in her teens when she was living in occupied Holland during World War II, so she had firsthand experience of childhood privation. Her memories of oppression, and the gratitude she felt upon liberation as well as the simple generosity of soldiers who handed her chocolate bars, would always stay with her and would fuel her passion for humanitarian work. She would say of the organization she devoted the last years of her life to, "… *I was among those who received food and medical relief right after World War II… I have a long-standing gratitude and trust for what UNICEF does.*"

She wasn't just paying lip service. Part of a UNICEF Global Ambassador's job, is to use their fame and platforms to bring attention to certain issues, or engage with key influencers and actors to create positive change. For Audrey Hepburn in the 1980s, this meant going around the world on missions to experience and understand what is happening in troubled locales, and then to bring the world's attention to it to create public awareness. For example, among her first trips in her new role was to Ethiopia, where she witnessed famine and draught amid civil strife. After her mission, she went around the United States, Canada and Europe, doing up to 15 interviews a day about her experiences. When she wasn't in the field, she was engaging with governments and participating in fundraising efforts, and would actually make several appearances at Congress as part of her advocacies.

She took her role – as she does any role be it in film or in real life – very seriously. She went to different countries for different programs and causes under UNICEF. She was in Turkey for a polio vaccine project, in

Ecuador for one focusing on street children and Guatemala for another working on improving access to drinking water. In Bangladesh she advocated for education while in Vietnam she did the same for proper nutrition, and in Sudan she looked into the plight of displaced children.

She kept busy with her advocacies right up until she found out she was ill. It's been reported that she started feeling abdominal pains in 1992, which was originally thought to be some kind of infection. She continued with her work either way, keeping her commitments in Somalia. But when she returned to the United States and underwent tests, the doctors eventually gave her a cancer diagnosis. Though she would have surgery to relieve the illness, the prognosis was unpromising. The cancer was quickly ravaging her body.

Before she died, her work with children was recognized with the Presidential Medal of Freedom – the highest award the United States can give to a civilian. She was also honored by the Academy Awards of 1993 with the Jean Hersholt Humanitarian Award; the announcement was made early in January, but Audrey Hepburn died that month in her sleep, and it would be accepted on behalf by her son, Sean Hepburn-Ferrer, in April later that year.

Audrey Hepburn is part of Hollywood's most elite list – the "EGOT Club." These are artists who have achieved Emmy, Grammy, Oscar and Tony wins along the course of their careers. Over Hollywood's lengthy history, there are only about a dozen people listed here. But for a beautiful woman with an enviable collection of gifts that would eventually garner her a coveted spot in this list, it must be remembered that at the height of her success, Audrey Hepburn was willing to walk away from it all. What she really wanted to do was to focus on her family, and the few instances that could draw her back into the public eye were her humanitarian work, the occasional compelling project, and tributes or events honoring those she worked with and loved. She was a woman in the best sense of the word. She was a lover and mother, a devoted friend, a fighter for those who could not stand up for themselves, and an inspiration for others to do the same. These are probably what she would consider her greatest achievements.

Audrey Hepburn's last role on screen, a small role in Steven Spielberg's *Always* (1989), is perhaps small but extremely fitting – she had played an angel.

Audrey Hepburn's Legacy

Audrey Hepburn is big business.

People's desire to forge a connection with her raises stunning sums at auction. Items include letters, photographs, clothes, scripts, jewelry and other memorabilia. And oh, what sums these items can command. In September, 2017, her shooting script of *Breakfast at Tiffany's* went for almost $850,000 at auction. Through online and live sales through London auction house Christie's, various items, including the said script, some jewelry, photos and (*of course!*) clothing, picked up over $6 million. The auction was made possible by her two sons, who wanted their mother's things to be able to fetch funds for her charitable causes, as well be put into the hands of people who continue to adore and appreciate her.

The guardians of Audrey Hepburn's name and likeness – her powerful brand - are Sean Hepburn-Ferrer, her only child from her first marriage with Mel; and Luca Dotti, her only child from her second marriage with Dr. Andrea Dotti. Any child may perhaps be considered the carrier of their parent's legacy, but in the case of these men and their late superstar mother, it is also a living. Audrey Hepburn, after all, has a seriously lucrative posthumous career.

Audrey Hepburn's name and likeness, still sells. It's not just about things she actually owned and touched while she was alive, as in the case of the items that have gone for auction. Decades after her most iconic works, and decades after her death, Audrey Hepburn's star still shines and is effective for use in advertising. Her very image, conveys beauty and style, yes, but more importantly, powerful femininity, class, and timeless grace. Her images appear for luxury timepiece brand Longines, accompanied by the copy, "*Elegance is an attitude.*" Her likeness was recreated in 2014 for a stunning and surprisingly lifelike Dove Chocolate / Galaxy television ad, asking, "*Why have cotton when you can have silk?*" In 2006, a Gap campaign to "*Keep it Simple*" included a TV commercial featuring clips of Audrey from *Funny Face*, to advertise the clothing company's classic, skinny black pants.

These are just a few of the ads that use her name and trademark image, whereas others settle for an invocation of her, through key elements of her iconic style. Fashion and entertainment magazines are particularly fond of doing this, dressing up today's stars in Audrey Hepburn-style garb, hair and makeup. Actress, comedian and bestselling writer Tina Fey appeared on the cover of *Entertainment Weekly* in full, Holly Golightly glory – LBD, elbow-length gloves, chignon, tiara, pearls, long cigarette holder and oh yes, a Cat. In 2006, Academy Award-winning actress, Natalie Portman, wore the original black Givenchy piece for a *Harper's Bazaar* cover. Another Academy Award-winning beauty, Anne Hathaway, channeled the icon in a shoot for *Vogue*.

These are, of course, by design. Sometimes, even when they don't intend to do it, comparisons to Audrey Hepburn are inevitable whenever a beautiful, young, stylish, elfin, waifish actress of some caliber and gravitas catches the world's attention. Natalie Portman, Emma Watson and Lily Collins all got that treatment. It's almost as if the world misses her terribly, and is in constant search for that Audrey Hepburn spirit in every promising actress who comes our way.

But there's simply more to Audrey Hepburn than meets the eye and that is probably why "the new" or "the next" Audrey is so hard to find. It is a spirit, a sense of something deeper and larger and more fundamental, but all the same something difficult to grasp and articulate. She was an Original. She had It, that X-factor, that strange, secret appeal.

Maybe it came from the vulnerabilities carved by her childhood – broken family, walkout father, parents who were not openly affectionate. Maybe it came from her experiences of war – the act she had to put up to help the Resistance, the secrets she had to keep to survive in an occupied country, the hunger and privation she had to suffer, the violence she saw on the streets, the homes she had to abandon in search of safety. Maybe it came from her failed relationships. Either way, all of these things came together to form a singular, profoundly appealing and unforgettable woman. All these hardships somehow made her strong and lovely and delightful, as if a series of wrongs could make a right.

If anyone can package that quality and sell it, they would be breaking the bank. In the meantime, it hasn't hurt companies to try, and they use invocations of her or her actual, trademarked image, to attempt to sell their goods and services. And make no mistake – her name is a brand and can in certain contexts, actually, *actually* come with a trademark sign.

The commercialization of her image has met with some criticism from certain purists and fans. It cheapens her likeness, some would say. She was a private person and so elegant and tasteful. Should you really have her image peddle chocolate and pants? How would she feel about that? Indeed, the protection of her image and legacy had even courted a recent set of controversies.

In 2017, there would be suits between her son, Sean Ferrer, and the charity established in her name. There were issues of who had unlimited rights to the use of the Audrey

Hepburn intellectual property, with or without the necessity of Sean and brother Luca's permissions. There were allegations that Sean had been interfering in their work, potentially damaging his own mother's reputation. Later that same year, Sean would be raising complaints of his own too, contesting that control and rights fell upon him and his brother as principal heirs, and expressing disapproval with how the some of the fund's activities went against Audrey's charitable intentions, including high administrative costs and executive salaries as well as insufficient percentages of proceeds used in charity work. These are just the barest details of the complaints and suits. It's a complex issue going into ownership of IP, and limitations on who and what can be used for what purpose, and how proceeds are to be spent.

Everyone just wants to be protective of Audrey Hepburn's legacy, and all claim to be selective in the use of her image and where they may appear and what they sell and stand for. Hopefully it is settled in the best possible way, not only for the preservation of Audrey Hepburn's image, but also for the children's charities that the fund - named for her and established by those who love her - supports. After all, for good or ill, her image still creates proceeds of which a large part is channeled into the Audrey Hepburn Children's Fund – and this is probably what would be most important for a humanitarian like Audrey Hepburn.

Bette Davis

A Bette Davis Biography

Katy Holborn

Copyright © 2017.

All rights reserved. No part of this publication may be reproduced, distributed, or transmitted in any form or by any means, including photocopying, recording, or other electronic or mechanical methods, without the prior written permission of the publisher, except in the case of brief quotations embodied in critical reviews and certain other noncommercial uses permitted by copyright law.

This book is intended for informational and entertainment purposes only. The publisher limits all liability arising from this work to the fullest extent of the law.

Table of Contents

No One Better Than Bette

Introduction

The First Lady of Film

Screen Queen Rising

Rebel Queen of the Screen

The Best of Bette

'The Lonely Life…'

"Ham" (married: 1932-1938)

Howard Hughes

William Wyler – The One That Got Away

Arthur Farnsworth (married: 1940-1943)

William Grant Sherry (married: 1945 – 1950)

Gary Merrill (married 1950-1960)

Franchot Tone: The Birth of a Feud

Bette Davis as a Mother

Legacy: Larger Than Life

No One Better Than Bette

Introduction

One of the greatest pop songs of all time, is about one of the greatest actresses of all time.

Bette Davis Eyes was written by Jackie DeShannon and Donna Weiss in 1974, and popularized by Kim Carnes in 1981. To say "popularized" may be an understatement – the song held the #1 spot at the *U.S. Billboard Hot 100* chart for nine weeks and stayed in the Top 40 for 20; it helped usher Kim Carnes' album sales up to a staggering eight million copies; and it won for the singer a Grammy Award for Record of the Year.

Its popularity was not just a passing thing, either. It was the third best-seller of the *entire* decade, where that decade – the 1980s – was one of the most important periods of music history. Over the years since its release, the beautiful song found life anew again and again. The Chipmunks gave it a shot in 1982, and Academy Award-winning actress, Gwyneth Paltrow, took it on in 2000 for her film, *Duets*. Pop and dance diva Kylie Minogue added her own spin in 2014, and 10-time Grammy Award winner, Country / Pop crossover star Taylor Swift, enjoyed doing a cover version before massive tour audiences in 2011.

The song, which repeats the line, "*She's got Bette Davis eyes*" over and over, speaks of an irresistible woman of playfulness, self-possession and intrigue – a woman whose "*hands are never cold,*" a woman who can "*make a pro blush,*" a woman who will "*Roll you like you were dice.*"

The imagery is vivid and powerful. Naturally, the songwriters have been asked about what compelled them to write this modern classic. To say the obvious answer, that the actress Bette Davis' titular prying peepers moved them to bring pen to paper, is inadequate; the woman, after all, worked in Hollywood for 50 years and had over 100 film credits to show for it. She started in film in the 1930s, and worked right up to the year of her death in 1989, at age 81. Which of her many incarnations moved them to write one of the greatest pop songs of all time?

Inspiration supposedly came after a viewing of the classic film, *Now, Voyager* (1942). The movie is centered on Charlotte Vale (played by Davis), a privileged but repressed spinster driven towards a nervous breakdown by her overbearing, tyrannical mother. Treatments at an institution transform her into a more chic and confident woman, who eventually finds forbidden romance with an unhappily married man, Jerry Durrance. By some reports, the songwriters of *Bette Davis Eyes* were drawn in by a particularly compelling scene, where Jerry lights two cigarettes at the same time and hands one to Charlotte. It was the film's signature moment, and a classic cinema moment all on its own.

Bette Davis was 73 years old when the hit song came out, and she reportedly wrote letters to Kim Carnes and the songwriters. In them, she is said to have expressed her appreciation of the song and its role in giving her such a place in modern history, and how she was grateful for how contemporary it made her seem to her grandchildren.

The letters suggest an unexpected, grounded quality in an otherwise proud, confident woman who should never have had any doubt of her permanent position in Hollywood's Parthenon of stars. She was, after all, an accomplished actress with double-digit nominations and two Oscar wins, an Academy Awards record holder for most consecutive acting nominations (alongside Greer Garson), and the first female president of the Academy in 1941 (however short her term had been – for Bette's exits always were as dramatic as her entrances).

She had also become the queen of camp and a beloved icon for the gay community; the subject of many a documentary and biography (including a bestselling, scathing, relationship-ending one by her own daughter); and an off-screen life so fitting to her outsize screen presence that even just a small part of it (her rivalry with fellow screen legend Joan Crawford) is worthy of a hit television series like the recent *Feud* (2017).

She is so striking that her name isn't just on the title of one of the biggest hits of all time – *Bette Davis Eyes* isn't even the first or the last song to mention it. Bette Davis is – just to mention a few - namedropped in iconic, trailblazing superstar Madonna's hit single, *Vogue*; in influential rock band The Kinks' *Celluloid Heroes*; in hit pop-punk band, Good Charlotte's *Silver Screen Romance*; in boy band LFO's *The Girl on TV*; and in Grammy,

Golden Globe, Oscar *and* Nobel Prize-winning artist, Bob Dylan's *Desolation Row*.

When great things are expected from a person, the commonly used phrase is something to the effect of – 'One day, they will write songs about you.' In the case of Bette Davis, she has had more than her fair share of tributes and it is of no surprise; few actors have her ability to captivate and inspire, her courage to challenge, and her willingness to repulse and terrify an audience in the name of her craft. Because here in Hollywood, even if she were in a town of giants, she was an unapologetic titan.

The First Lady of Film

Ruth Elizabeth Davis was born on the 5th of April 1908, to parents Ruth Favor Davis and Harlow Morrell Davis, in Lowell, Massachusetts. When she was around 7 or 8 years old, her parents divorced and her father, a Harvard Law graduate who became a patent lawyer for the government, left their mother to care for Bette and her younger sister, Barbara, all on her own. Ruthie, as Mrs. Davis was known, did everything she could to send Bette and Barbara to a boarding school in New England, reportedly even doing some cleaning work.

Bette attended her mother's alma mater, the Cushing Academy in Massachusetts. She showed an early interest and aptitude for the performing arts. She started with dance, but eventually found the call of theater irresistible. She featured in productions at school and when she graduated, she aimed for the prestigious dramatic schools of New York City.

She was 19 years old, and her first stop was to actress Eva Le Gallienne's Manhattan Civic Repertory in 1927. Not only was she rejected from admittance, she reportedly left having been told that she was *"a frivolous little girl"* with an insincere attitude for the theater! It was quite the verdict, especially as Bette Davis would eventually be known for her on-screen and off-screen theatricality, her joy and devotion for working, and for her courage to take on roles that would have sent any other actresses scurrying away in fear.

A scathing initial rejection was fitting to the Bette Davis narrative, anyway. Her off-screen theatricality was long-established, even before she studied to become an actress. She was born, they say, with a background of lightning and thunder. She had a flair for drama even as a child, when she detested dolls, chopped off her younger sister's beautiful hair, and once reportedly pretended to be blind. She even had a sense of showmanship when it came to her name. She took on the rarer "Bette" as opposed to "Betty" around 1917, based on the suggestion of one of her mother's friends to adopt a change inspired by French author Honoré de Balzac's novel "Cousin Bette." Bette Davis was reportedly convinced that making a small difference in her name can better set her apart.

Her childhood experiences had plenty of fodder for more serious dramatics too, what with her father Harlow and her mother Ruthie's poor relationship. Harlow reportedly did not even want to have Bette, fearing that he and his wife did not have the financial means to become parents at the time Ruthie became pregnant. He even ate separately from his wife and two children, from whom he reportedly had slim reserves of patience. He eventually left them in 1915 and Bette had reportedly always looked upon the divorce a kind of abandonment.

Thus, even at her young age, Bette Davis had a lot of experience and strength to draw from, as well as a devoted and ambitious mother ready to spur her forward. Undeterred by her crushing rejection at the hands of Le Gallienne, Bette managed to secure admission to the John Murray Anderson / Robert Milton School of Theater and Dance, also in New York City. One of her instructors would later describe her as having control and electricity. The storied school counts another legend amongst its alumni – Lucille Ball. She and Bette Davis were classmates there.

Bette Davis paid her theater dues, doing summer stock in Rochester, Upstate New York. But she was quickly crawling her way towards The Great White Way. By 1929, she was in the off-Broadway play, *The Earth Between* at the Provincetown Playhouse in Greenwich Village. It was an important, busy time for the actress. Soon she was also on stage in Ibsen's *The Wild Duck*, and then making her Broadway debut at the age of 21 for *Broken Dishes*. She was an electrifying performer, and would get notice for her debut, as well as for another Broadway appearance, in *Solid South*.

It wasn't long before Hollywood – at the cusp of its Golden Age after the release of talkies, and eager for talents trained in speaking and singing from the theater - came knocking at her door.

Screen Queen Rising

Bette Davis was not a conventional beauty.

She was 5'3", slight, pop-eyed, almost cartoony. She would eventually acquire the nickname, 'little brown wren' in a town of more finely-feathered beauties. Her peers, for example, included Hollywood heavyweights Marlene Dietrich (born 1901), Greta Garbo (born 1905), Joan Crawford (born 1905), Katherine Hepburn (born 1907), and Carole Lombard (born 1908).

When Sam Goldwyn saw her screen test, he was reportedly aghast. But the folks over at Universal Pictures had more vision. By the end of 1930, with less than $100 in their pockets, Bette and her mother, Ruthie (along with their pet terrier), took the leap and headed to Hollywood. She would stay in the entertainment industry for the rest of her life, but no one would have known it on her arrival, or on her initial, forgettable appearances in the movies.

According to Hollywood lore, literally from the time she arrived, she was so unlike the preconceived idea of a movie star that the studio representative assigned to meet her at the train station was not able to find her. At the time, Universal officials who encountered her were unimpressed by her looks and her sex appeal. She got a makeover, but would be tossed into relatively minor roles in unimpressive films. In 1931, she appeared in *Way Back Home* (her debut), as well as *Waterloo Bridge*, *The Bad Sister* and *Seed*.

Her contract wouldn't be renewed and she was getting ready to leave Hollywood and return to the East coast. But her talent was apparent to distinguished Academy Award-winning actor, George Arliss, who at the time was with Warner Brothers and on the lookout for a fine young actress to star with in *The Man Who Played God* (1932). Later, she would say how she initially refused to believe that the famed Mr. Arliss was seeking her out for a role. Thankfully, she took a chance and when she signed on for the role of Grace Blair, Hollywood would never be the same - it was the role that would keep her in town.

The Man Who Played God is based on the play, *The Silent Voice*. It is about a gifted musician deafened during a performance where there was an assassination attempt on his royal audience. The loss of his senses and the consequent decline of his career proved devastating, but with his loyal fiancée by his side, he learned to cope and channel his talents to philanthropic activities. It was made as a silent film featuring Arliss a decade earlier; a practice he'd done before, as when he made a silent and sound film for *Disraeli* (1921 and 1929) and *The Green Goddess* (1923 and 1930).

Mr. Arliss lent gravitas to many a Hollywood picture, and Bette Davis would always credit him for her big break. The distinguished veteran also helped her with technique and character development, and they would work together again for *The Working Man* (1933). The admiration was mutual; he would write about her literally in glowing terms for his 1940 autobiography, describing the 'illuminating flash' and light she could give to words.

Bette signed a multi-year deal with Warner Brothers, and from 1932 to 1934, she made 14 movies, many of them very successful. She would also be known for her powerful performance of complex characters.

It's that gift that would bring her to RKO for *Of Human Bondage* (1934), a role she had pressed studio boss Jack Warner to give her the chance to portray. Warner Bros. loaned her to the rival studio to play the strong-willed, selfish, hateful, vulgar vixen, Mildred Rogers, for a film based on the novel by W. Somerset Maugham. Critics and audiences were enthralled. Bette Davis could play a theoretically unsympathetic character, but still get people on her side. Over the course of her career, her most memorable roles would find her boldly walking that thin, high line – she could be selfish, mean and even villainous, but a leading lady and heroine all the same.

Many young (and even established) actors would have feared such a brand, but Bette Davis could be fearless with her craft. She was unafraid of looking unattractive for the right part. She did not fear being typecast as a villain; she was confident in her own range and besides, as she would later say, they "*…always have the best-written parts.*" And Bette Davis was the best actress to utter them.

Of Human Bondage was a turning point for the actress. Audiences, critics, studios and peers were now paying the rising star rapt attention, and she would be rewarded for her bold performance with her first Academy Award nomination as a write-in nominee.

Bette Davis was not officially nominated for an Academy Award for her performance, and the oversight was received poorly. The cause may have been that she was on loan for *Of Human Bondage,* and so there wasn't much incentive for RKO (which made the film) or Warner (which loaned her out) to promote her performance as Oscar-worthy. There would be claims that Jack Warner may have even campaigned against her, but there is no readily available proof to substantiate this.

Either way, following the scandal over her snub in the Best Actress category, the Academy permitted write-in candidates. It is the first time of only two years that write-in nominations would be allowed. In a way, this is one of the moments that showed how her outsize talent can overwhelm an institution. Bette Davis was the exception rather than the rule.

She lost out to Claudette Colbert of *It Happened One Night,* but she had a very acceptable 'consolation prize' – the accolade put her in a position to command better, more compelling roles. By 1935, she would be walking away with the coveted golden statuette for *Dangerous*.

Rebel Queen of the Screen

Bette Davis top-billed *Dangerous* in the role of struggling actress Joyce Heath, an alcoholic desperate for a comeback. Her redeemer comes in the form of Don Bellows, played by patrician actor, Franchot Tone on loan from MGM (an on loan from his then-fiancée, actress Joan Crawford – but more on this scandal, later). Salvation for the embattled Heath, however, came at the cost of something she was not free to give – marriage. She copes poorly against this dilemma to disastrous results, but finds redemption in paying the consequences of her actions.

It was not considered a stellar script, and Davis had actually been hesitant to take it on. Studio production head Hal Wallis, however, gave her creative heart a boost by his trust that she could make the role special, and added the incentive of engaging two of Warner's top behind-the-scenes talents, Ernest Haller and Orry-Kelly. Haller's (a cameraman) and Kelly's (a costume designer) aesthetic aligned with Davis' brutally realistic vision of an actress in decline.

This is exemplified in the scene when a down-and-out Joyce Heath is found by Don Bellows in a rundown bar. The strong-willed Davis is said to have encountered similarly troubled women when she was in theater, and wanted to convey that gritty realism for her character. The end result was Haller's camera playing it straight, with little regard for flattering angles or lighting. The costume designer, Kelly, on the other hand, dressed the character in simple, aged clothes.

Attention to detail and an electrifying performance by Davis gave the film a winning, grounded vision, and Davis took home the Academy Award for Best Actress in a Leading Role in 1936. The Oscar made her a legitimate star and the reigning "queen" over at Warner Bros.

At a time when studios held so much control over actors though, "Queen" was a relative term. She was referred to as such when her image was sold for a Quaker Puffed Rice advertisement that was printed alongside the line, "*A Breakfast fit for a Queen of the Screen...*" But the award did not really help her progress towards the kinds of material and meaningful roles that she has grown to enjoy and crave – at least, not without her putting up a fight.

In the months following her Oscar win, she was suspended for declining a role. Again, at a time when studios held such power over the industry, actors were expected to toe the line and play whatever was demanded of them - or risk suspension without pay and without the freedom to work anywhere else. Bette Davis took the suspension and headed to Europe hoping to work there, but Warner Bros. was hot on her heels with a contract and the power of the law. She would lose the suit, but return to Hollywood with a louder voice the studio now knew they had to take more seriously. The parts sent her way improved and so did her pay. The trailblazing actress had broken the rules again, only to be rewarded for her efforts.

The Best of Bette

In Bette Davis' extensive filmography, her most important roles include her breakthrough performance with George Arliss in *The Man Who Played God* (1932) – it kept her in Hollywood and gave her another chance at Warner Bros. Then there was *Of Human Bondage* (1934), which had the industry watching and holding their breaths for what she would be able to do next. With *Dangerous* (1935) she had secured her Oscar, and it gave her courage and leverage to buck against the studio system for better roles and better pay. *Now, Voyager* (1942) was so moving it inspired a pop song that brought a then-aging, living legend into modern history. Many other roles would constitute her best work:

- In *The Petrified Forest* (1936), she plays a dreamer diner girl, Gabrielle Maple, who longs for excitement She had Paris in mind, but excitement nevertheless finds her when a dejected writer, Alan Squier (played by Leslie Howard) graces her workplace shortly before the fugitive Duke Mantee (Humphrey Bogart) takes it over. She is off-type here, but still a gifted actress at an intriguing time in her development, as it shows her growing sense of presence and confidence on the screen.

- *Marked Woman* (1937) had her playing Mary Strauber, a hostess at a nightclub who decides to testify against her gangster employer. The consequences of her decision is a brutal beating that leaves her disfigured – a gutsy move on the part of Davis, at a time when beautiful screen imagery was the norm for actresses. Throughout her career, she never feared showing flaw or age or later, even sheer grotesqueness in her face, if she thought it was meaningful to a character. She was unafraid of being perceived as flawed or even ugly as early as the 1930s, but would carry that commitment over to when she shaved her hairline playing Queen

Elizabeth I in *The Private Lives of Elizabeth and Essex* (1939) and *The Virgin Queen* (1955); in *Mrs. Skeffington* (1944) where she showed age, hair-loss and illness; and of course in *Whatever Happened to Baby Jane?* (1962) in her most grotesque, cakey make-up incarnation.

- In *Jezebel* (1938), Bette Davis acted out her Scarlett O'Hara frustrations and blew everyone away as Julie Marston. Davis had wanted badly to play the fiery, irrepressible lead of David O. Selznick's upcoming *Gone with the Wind* (1939), but a deal to loan her out – which included Errol Flynn as Rhett Butler - didn't pan out. *Jezebel* was a fair substitute that shared some of *Gone with the Wind's* attributes – self-absorbed, hard-headed Southern Belle falls in love, loses love, finds personal strength and redemption. *Jezebel* wasn't quite as epic or sweeping, but it is still a classic and it did get five well-deserved Academy Award nominations, including a second Best Actress win for Bette Davis. The role would also get her rave reviews, a cover on *Time* magazine, and a great love affair with acclaimed director, William Wyler.

- Judith Traherne of *Dark Victory* (1939) is said to have been one of Bette Davis' favorite parts, for it allowed her to display the range of her considerable talents. She starts as a radiant, carefree socialite whose world turns upside down when diagnosed with an inoperable brain tumor. She decides to live her life fully, to pursue happiness, to give and take love…

but is always shadowed by what's to come. It was a tour de force worthy of another Oscar nomination – except that year, the award would be brought home by Vivien Leigh, the stunning and talented actress who secured the role of Scarlett O'Hara in *Gone with the Wind*. Fans of Bette Davis can't help but wonder at what Bette Davis could have done with the irresistible Scarlett if she had only been given the chance.

- After the success of *Jezebel,* Wyler and Davis made film magic anew in the film noir classic, *The Letter* (1940). Bette plays Leslie Crosby, adulterous wife to the administrator of a rubber plantation. It opens with a merciless Leslie pumping bullets on her lover and later claiming self-defense – an excuse threatened by a letter that could expose her lies. Theoretically, Leslie isn't a sympathetic character, but Davis is captivating in how she infuses the character with complexity. She was just as compelling in her last collaboration with Wyler, for *The Little Foxes* in 1941. In it, she plays the selfish Regina, who was not above using her own family for her nefarious purposes. In one key scene, she coldly watches her dying husband trying to crawl up a flight of stairs for his medicines. She was chilling and irresistible to watch.

Throughout her career, Bette Davis held such passion for her work. According to her, beyond life's disappointments, work is that one thing which "*really stands by a human being.*" She would also be quoted for statements like "*it is only work that truly satisfies*" or that she felt a profound, sweet joy "*at the end of a good day's work.*" In her later years when she fell gravely ill, she was open about the sheer "*terror*" at the prospect of never being able to work again, when it was that one thing that she "*always very much loved.*"

That value she placed on her profession was reflected in her constant drive to keep performing. In one interview, she had claimed that one of the things she feared was a fate like that of a faded star who needed to auction off her things, and so she did not like owning things that couldn't fit in a trunk. And so, on and on she worked, almost right up until the end of her life.

Her two Oscars and string of hits had made her the Queen over at Warners when she was just in her early 30 years of age, but even good things must come to an end. Critical and commercial disappointments during the 1940s, including *Deception* (1946) which had reportedly lost money, ultimately led to her studio releasing her in 1949 after 19 years of keeping her under contract. Bette wouldn't be down for very long, though, and soon, she would be wowing the town again in Mankiewicz's *All About Eve* (1950):

- Bette Davis got 10 Best Actress Oscar nominations in her life, but Joseph L. Mankiewicz's *All About Eve*, for which she was of course nominated, is probably where she played her most memorable role and uttered her most iconic line –

"Fasten your seatbelts. It's going to be a bumpy night." The part of Margo Channing actually wasn't meant for her – she was a replacement for Claudette Colbert, who had been injured. But the character Margo, a theater star under threat from an interloping former fan overly eager to take over her personal and professional life, was characterized by Davis so indelibly that it is now difficult to imagine the role being played by anyone else.

Bette Davis' career had a brief resurgence after she brought the unforgettable Margo Channing to the screen, and she played the lead in *The Star* (1952). In this movie, Davis plays a down-and-out, award-winning actress, Margaret Elliott, whose star has faded. She was no longer working in film and she has become mired in legal and financial troubles. She has a chance at love and a new life, but still struggles to reclaim the glories of her old one. The film was supposedly about Bette Davis' Hollywood rival, Joan Crawford… which was reportedly one of the reasons why it had been appealing to Bette Davis!

The First Lady of Film again found herself in the Oscar race for Best Actress, but the movie did not perform to expectations at the box office. Bette Davis would then appear in few other major screen projects throughout the fifties. But Bette was a true artist with a work ethic to match, and she found other outlets for her gift and love of performance. She diversified the media where she shared her talent. After finishing her work on *The Star*, she headed back to Broadway for *Two's Company*, which opened in December, 1952 and closed in March, 1953 after just 90 performances; it received poor critical reception. She also lent her talents to television. While some of her peers had been skeptical of the medium, Bette was an early adapter and made numerous appearances in several TV series throughout the decade.

It was a light ten years compared to her previous outputs, and it was during this era in her life that she actually found time to be a wife and a mother. Earlier in the decade, she became romantically involved with and eventually married her *All About Eve* co-star, Gary Merrill. For a few of her work's quiet years, she could devote herself to family. Unfortunately, she later claimed it was when

Gary fell out of love for her. The couple went on tour performing on *The World of Carl Sandburg*, but their marriage was already on shaky ground. In 1960 they divorced, and the play made its way to Broadway without Merrill. It opened in September, 1960 and closed in October, 1960 after only 29 performances. She eventually had a longer running show, with Tennessee Williams' *The Night of the Iguana*, which opened in December, 1961. But the real monster hit of the decade for Davis was the movie, *What Ever Happened to Baby Jane?*

- Director Robert Aldrich's *Whatever Happened to Baby Jane?* (1962) brought storied rivals, Bette Davis and Joan Crawford together on screen for their *only* film together. The psychological thriller has Davis playing Jane, a former child star ruined by a lost career, drink, and worsening mental illness. Crawford plays Jane's older sister Blanche, a wheelchair-bound former Hollywood actress. The sisters have a claustrophobic, co-dependent relationship, with an immobile Blanche completely reliant on Jane, while Jane is financially at the mercy of Blanche, burdened by her care, and tortured by her own demons. They are so hopelessly tied together, even as their bonds run with long-standing resentment and jealousy. As Jane descends further into madness, she cruelly drags her sister down with her in increasingly sadistic acts gradually escalating to the point of murder. Bette Davis is horrifying and so intentionally grotesque in this piece of Hollywood gothic, and her turn as Jane got her yet another Academy Award nomination, the last of her life. The campy spectacle was a big hit, which gave a boost to the two actress's flailing careers.

And so, with a big hit in her hands, Bette Davis was able to continue with her beloved work. She took on leads and she took on character roles. She performed in a variety of genres, but found a particular home in melodramas and thrillers. At one point, she had even donned an eye patch for *The Anniversary* (1968). She appeared in both movies and in television. She would even pick up an Emmy in 1979 as Outstanding Lead Actress in a Limited Series or a Special, for *Strangers: The Story of a Mother and Daughter*.

She really came to embrace the medium of television. Television embraced her back. The peak of her popularity may have been in Hollywood's Golden Age from the 1930s to the early 1950s, but Bette Davis was a frequent presence on small screens all over the country, via made-for-TV movies, TV shows, and repeat showings of her classic films. In this way, she had become a star across media and a star across generations.

It wasn't always easy for Bette Davis, though. She always had to fight for her place in the limelight. She was an intelligent woman with self-awareness about this too. Later in life, she conceded that she had on occasion been rude, insufferable and uncompromising… because she "*had no time for pleasantries.*"

When she first came to Hollywood, she fought to get a contract. She fought to stay employed. Once employed, she fought for more creative control and better pay. When she reached the top, she fought to stay there. As her stature waned, she fought for parts. As her health declined, she fought against her own body to continue working.

After she died, she was buried in Los Angeles with a tombstone that reads, "*She did it the hard way.*" But she had to; she was tough and she was a fighter, and she bucked and kicked with everything she had. She used her talents, she used her smarts, she used that unassailable, quick-wit, and she fought with ballsy nerve.

In the 1960s, for example, after filming wrapped on *What Ever Happened to Baby Jane?* but before it came out as a massive hit, she may have worried for what the future held for her… enough that she had taken out a newspaper ad for her services! Among the choice lines was, "…*Mobile still and more affable than rumor would have it. Wants steady employment in Hollywood…*"

It was classic Bette Davis; whip-smart and biting, with dark humor and a dash of commentary. Hollywood observers note that she probably wasn't in such desperate straits to need an ad like this, but in a way it was a critique of an industry that was taking her talent and years of service for granted, and of how there were such limited opportunities available for older women in Hollywood.

And then, *What Ever Happened to Baby Jane* came out to punctuate her point. There was still a place for a performer of her caliber in entertainment. What she did not know at the time, is that there would *always* be a place for her in entertainment.

She was also aware however, that her devotion to work came at the cost of other things – most painfully, her failed romances and troubled family life.

'The Lonely Life…'

Just as the historical Queen Elizabeth I was married to England (a character she would portray on film twice), Bette Davis, Queen of Hollywood, was "The First Lady of Film." She was a woman married to the movies. Work seemed to be her only lasting partner, for she would have trouble being a "first lady" to anyone else.

Bette Davis, according to some Hollywood commentators, may have been handicapped by her harsh experiences with her distant, disapproving father. It had a negative impact on her relationships, but then again, so could have many other factors, including how focused she was on her career; how little time she could devote to her relationships;

and how her men were able to cope with her fierce personality, hectic lifestyle, the spotlight on their life, and her greater success compared to their own.

For Bette Davis, work always seemed to come first, but she was also a woman who liked men, had confessed to an appetite for sex, and craved companionship. Sometimes, her professional and personal needs just couldn't complement each other, resulting in a string of husbands and broken relationships.

"Ham" (married: 1932-1938)

Bette first found love with Harmon Oscar Nelson Jr. – the "Ham" (as she called him) to her "Spuds" (as he called her). They were together during their time at Cushing Academy, and they married at Yuma in 1932.

He was a moderately successful musician and bandleader, and he and Bette would have long spells apart when he toured with an orchestra and when she was immersed in the demands of her own work.

When they divorced, he claimed that she neglected him in pursuit of her career. The end of their six-year marriage, however, would be plagued by harsher tales too. It couldn't have been easy if he was, as has been reported, lampooned for allegedly earning a tenth of what she was making. There were also allegations of physical abuse, and claims of multiple abortions done at his behest so as not to disrupt the trajectory of her career and the momentum of her success. Then there were also reports of Bette's affair with notorious moneyman Howard Hughes...

Howard Hughes

The Hollywood power player, multi-millionaire lothario was linked to a bevy of greats, among them Ava Gardner, Olivia de Havilland and Rita Hayworth... but he reportedly told Bette Davis (whether sincerely or as a gimmick), that she was the only one who could help him climax. It had the desired effect, and he landed another legendary conquest. But the ever-witty dame harbored no illusions about the claim and had been quoted as saying, *"it was cheaper than buying gifts."*

According to one account, he and Bette had their dalliances when her husband Ham was away. When Ham found out, he allegedly had the erring pair monitored by a private eye, documented their affair, and threatened to make it publicly known. There were wild tales of a hit placed and retracted on Ham, and of big pay-offs in exchange for destroyed recordings. Divorce and leaving the marriage with a considerable share of his wife's assets, seems almost sedate compared to lore like this.

Around the time that all the drama was unfolding, Bette was also busy working on *Jezebel*, and ensnaring another major Hollywood figure – the director, William Wyler.

William Wyler – The One That Got Away

Newly-divorced, Hollywood director William Wyler first came into Bette Davis' life when he helmed *Jezebel*. Wyler was an artist and perfectionist, whose insistence on take after take after take would bring the picture behind schedule and over budget, but to stunning results. He was a strong personality with vision, and Bette not only stood up for him when the studio executives became dissatisfied by his performance, she also gave him her professional commitment… as well as her heart.

Not right away, of course, and not easily (this was, after all, Bette Davis). They had extended battles of wills on set, and she would repeatedly counter whatever direction he gave her before following. They found each other brilliant and irresistible. Eventually, under Wyler's direction, she was able to refine her techniques and churn out some of the greatest work of her life, as was the case in *Jezebel,* and later in *The Letter* (1940) and *The Little Foxes* (1941).

They had a passionate affair that is said to have resulted in a pregnancy that Bette felt compelled to abort, so as not to force William into a tenuous position. He reportedly asked her to marry him at one point, but she demurred and played hard to get, which she would come to regret later when he ended up marrying someone else. She always considered him the great love of her life, though Wyler wouldn't be as effusive; he found her too intense and emotional.

Arthur Farnsworth (married: 1940-1943)

Arthur Farnsworth has been described as a former commercial airline pilot, aircraft engineer and innkeeper. Most people, however, would know him best as the second husband of Bette Davis, most distinguishable amongst the lineup for his mysterious death.

Farnsworth and Davis knew each other in high school, and when they married in 1940, it was a surprise to most. They were together up until he died amid strange circumstances in 1943, and the actress was reportedly in such a hysterical state over the tragedy that she had to be placed under the care of a physician.

The circumstances around his passing remain clouded by questions. Farnsworth was reportedly found unconscious along Hollywood Boulevard and would pass away a few days later. He had apparently collapsed, and an autopsy would later reveal that the sidewalk fall came as a result of dizziness induced by pressure from a blood clot in his head. The blood clot was the result of a skull injury taken before the final fall.

Bette Davis was interrogated as a routine part of the ensuing investigation, and she revealed that her husband had taken a stair fall weeks earlier, while running to answer the phone. That injury was considered the cause of the clot. In a later theory, it has been suggested that Farnsworth may have been struck behind the head after he was discovered with his attacker's wife. Either way – Arthur Farnsworth died at the young age of 35, from the complications and belated effects of a head injury.

William Grant Sherry (married: 1945 – 1950)

Bette Davis next found love after World War II, in muscular ex-Marine, William Grant

Sherry. Sherry has been described as an artist, landscape artist, and masseur. When they met, he reportedly did not know who she was!

Troubles for the couple reportedly started early; he allegedly threw a trunk at her during their honeymoon. It wouldn't be the only thing he would throw at Bette; an ice bucket was said to be amongst the projectiles lobbed the actress' way.

Davis and Sherry had a child a few years after their wedding, Barbara Davis "B.D." Sherry, when Bette was 39. A child, however, couldn't save the marriage. Relations did not improve between husband and wife, and the couple divorced after five years together. The parting was, again, not without controversy; Mr. Sherry ended up marrying B.D.'s nanny, Marion Richards.

This difficult period in Bette's life also coincided with troubles in her career. A series of disappointing releases ended Bette's 19-year stint at Warners in 1949.

Gary Merrill (married 1950-1960)

For Bette, the new stage in her career led to a new stage in her love life too.

Bette Davis worked with actor Gary Merrill in the hit, *All About Eve*. They married just a few weeks after her divorce with William Grant Sherry was finalized in mid-1950. They adopted a baby girl shortly afterwards and named her Margot Mosher Merrill. The couple later adopted another child, whom they named Michael.

Merrill and Davis remained with each other for a while. He was the last of her husbands, and they stayed together for the longest time, from 1950 to 1960. Because her career was winding down in the 1950s, she also got to play a more domestic role in her marriage. They even lived in a farm in Maine with B.D. and their two kids.

Unfortunately for Bette, her domestic life still didn't work out. Their first adopted child was diagnosed with developmental issues and had to be sent away for care in a handicapped home. Gary's macho streak couldn't have been too helpful either; he was said to be a mean drunk who was rude to guests and willing to batter his wife.

It may seem uncharacteristic how the fiery Davis tolerated such treatment for so long, until we get a better idea of the larger battle she may have been fighting at the time; she wasn't just sticking around for the love of Gary. By some accounts, she was looking at this last marriage as a final chance at love, and an indicator of whether or not she could be a wife. By 1960 she conceded failure and they parted ways.

Later in life though, she came to realize that her failed efforts at being a wife were not wholly her fault. Of Gary and her husbands, she would say that no one seemed *"man enough to become Mr. Bette Davis…"*

Looking back at all the accomplishments of her life and long career – she was probably right!

Franchot Tone: The Birth of a Feud

In some ways, one of the longest relationships Bette Davis was able to keep was with fellow Hollywood legend, Joan Crawford. Unfortunately, it was more a feud than a friendship, and would last longer than whatever she had with most of the men who had come into her colorful life.

Surprisingly, Bette and Joan had a lot in common; they were both tough, pragmatic, modern and sensual. They had a string of love affairs and marriages, and notoriously troubled relationships with their children. But at one point in their lives, they shared something that precluded them from ever being friendly – an interest in actor, Franchot Tone, an MGM player famous for the hit, *Mutiny on the Bounty* (1935).

He was Bette Davis' leading man in *Dangerous*, and she is said to have fallen for the well-brought-up, Cornell-educated, New Yorker. Her marriage with Ham was not doing well at the time and she ended up having a big crush on her co-star. Later, she would say that while she had a personal and professional admiration for Tone, it was unrequited (this would be contested by allegations that the two actually did have an affair). She would even be reported as confessing to jealously watching as he and Joan Crawford, with whom he was engaged at the time, met daily for lunch. Tone and Crawford married in 1935 shortly after the filming wrapped, but divorced after four years.

Whether or not he and Bette actually had a fling or something more than a fling is unknown, especially as there would be conflicting accounts even from Bette herself. Decades after Davis and Tone starred together in 1935, her story changed. The shift has been attributed to either honesty from old age or illness, or an illusion, or an act. Either way, she reportedly claimed in 1987 that she would never forgive Crawford for ruthlessly taking Tone away from her.

Whatever it was that they had (if they had anything at all), the Davis-Tone link ended quickly, and would be long outlived by the legendary feud it allegedly sparked. The two women would have multiple run-in's in a town that gradually became too small for two screen queens.

Davis reportedly disliked Crawford and alleged that Crawford used sex to move forward in her career. During the Oscars ceremony when Bette won the Best Actress nod for *Dangerous*, for example, she reportedly did not expect to win and did not even want to go, so she arrived in a simple dress for the affair. After she won, Tone embraced her warmly, but had to prompt his new wife, Joan Crawford, to attention. Crawford, resplendent in her high formals, reportedly dryly commented on Bette's *"lovely frock."*

When Bette Davis' Hollywood fortunes started to diminish in the mid to late 1940s, Crawford (formerly of MGM) moved in on Davis' Warner Bros. territory; she secured the dressing room next to Bette's. By some reports it was not an altogether antagonistic move, and Crawford was said to have tried to initiate a truce with gifts and flowers.

Bette didn't bite though, and when one of Crawford's first major efforts for her new home, *Mildred Pierce* (1945), won her an Oscar and a lucrative contract, it didn't please the beleaguered Warners queen either. It probably did not help that the role was one Bette had allegedly turned down!

The heated rivalry between Bette Davis and Joan Crawford became part of Hollywood lore. Sometimes they perpetuated it by their comments against each other, and other times they doused it in saccharine denial. There was also a surprising twist to this tale. If true, Crawford, who is said to have indulged her sensuality with both men and women, might have actually felt an attraction or curiosity for Bette Davis.

The decades' old tension – whether it stemmed from a man, sexual attraction, or professional rivalry - boiled over when the two women were cast to play dysfunctional sisters in the psychological thriller, *What Ever Happened to Baby Jane?*

The partnership was reportedly suggested by Joan Crawford, who had past history working with the director, Robert Aldrich in *Autumn Leaves* (1956). It was theoretically a marketable - if gimmicky – proposition, to cast the rivals in the perfect vehicle to bring their tension to the screen. Nothing about it was easy, though; from the sourcing of project backers to negotiating between the two divas, to dealing with their on-set tension and sometimes, outright antagonism.

It was hard to manage two women wrapped up in deep, long-standing, mutual dislike of each other, but at that point of their lives they were again rather similar - they were two gifted but aging actresses fighting to keep their place in Hollywood. The project pushed through, but in the tight quarters and constant company of a set, they had plenty of occasions to needle each other. Among the choice encounters?

A scene that called for fake physical violence apparently ended up with a real kick from Bette Davis' shoe to Crawford's head. Crawford retaliated by wearing weights for a scene where Bette's character had to drag her around; Davis hurt her back doing the heavy lifting.

When it came out, the bizarre movie was a hit. Davis and Crawford not only made a killing, they made a comeback and forged yet another place for themselves in Hollywood history. They were legends apart, yes, but they were legends anew together.

Not that the film's success did anything to mend fences. Davis was nominated for a Best Actress award at the Oscars and Crawford was not; but Crawford had arranged to accept the Oscar for another nominee, Anne Bancroft. When Bancroft triumphed over Davis, it was Crawford holding the statuette that had escaped her. Crawford had also been accused of campaigning against her co-star.

Bette Davis' next major film, *Hush, Hush, Sweet Charlotte* (1964) with the same director, Robert Aldrich, was originally meant to reunite the rivals. However, Crawford eventually bowed out due to illness… if she was really gravely ill or not is uncertain, but it certainly couldn't have been encouraging when Davis allegedly arranged for the cast and crew to pose for a photograph with Coca-Cola – the chief competition of Pepsi Co., the company run by Crawford's late husband, Alfred Steele, and where she had been a spokesperson and board member. It wasn't the first time Bette Davis allegedly used soda to needle Crawford; if Hollywood lore is to be believed, she's once asked for a Coke machine in her dressing room on the set of *What Ever Happened to Baby Jane*, too.

At the time of this writing, it's been decades since both women's deaths – Crawford passed away in 1977 and Bette died in 1989 - but their storied rivalry only added to their individual magnetism. The strife between the two women would be reintroduced to contemporary audiences via the Ryan Murphy-helmed hit television series, *Feud* (2017).

Thus, as surely as *Bette Davis Eyes* brought Davis into the 1980s, a new generation met her acquaintance yet again.

Bette Davis as a Mother

The two women had several similarities, but the most glaring one was probably their difficult relationships with their children.

When Joan Crawford died, she had disinherited her adopted children, Christina and Christopher. About a year afterwards, Christina released the savage tell-all, *Mommie Dearest*, depicting Joan as an abusive, sadistic, drunk. The shocking revelations included Crawford's severe aversion to wire hangers and beating her child with one; other instances of physical abuse; starvation as punishment; and getting tied up in bed.

Whether completely factual or not – for a number of accounts would later contest some of the claims – *Mommie Dearest* made for truly compelling reading and was so cinematic it yielded a Faye Dunaway starrer, a film of the same name in 1981. Shelves would also be stocked with updated editions on its 20th and 30th-year anniversaries, showing continuing relevance for years to come.

Bette Davis was still very much alive and active in the industry when the book about her great rival came out. She has been quoted as saying Crawford did not deserve such a detestable act from someone she had saved from being an orphan. She went on to say that she felt sorry for Crawford, but understood that her rival wouldn't want her of all people to feel pity. She then said the pain would be "*Unimaginable*" if her daughter, B.D., submitted her to the same situation…

… and indeed, she wouldn't have had to imagine it at all.

In 1985, B.D. Hyman published *My Mother's Keeper* about her own difficulties with her mom, Bette. It was poorly received, what with Bette still alive and in frail health. Bette

Davis had previously suffered a broken hip, a mastectomy and a stroke, so Hyman's timing was regarded as somewhat cruel. B.D., however, would claim purer motivations; she said she had been trying to reach out to her mother but was ignored, so she brought her issues before the public so that Davis may finally acknowledge them. Whatever her motivations were, her revelations were rough too.

Bette was depicted as a heavy drinker, who referred to her handicapped child, Margot, as *"retarded."* She was shown as a mentally cruel, overly possessive egomaniac, and an embittered man-hater who discouraged ties between B.D. and her father, William Grant Sherry. There were even claims of how Bette had tried to sabotage the relationship between B.D. and the man who would be her husband.

The backlash was severe, and B.D. would get it even from familial quarters. Her adoptive brother, Michael Merrill, cut ties with her. Bette cut B.D. and her children, Ashley and Justin Hyman, from her will, too. And it was very unfortunate, considering Bette had harbored such hopes for B.D. and after her, her grandson Ashley as well. When he was 11 years old, she helped him get cast in a project with her. Reports indicate she treated her grandson as a professional, and was pleased by his potential, just as she had been pleased by B.D. when the young girl played a bit part in *What Ever Happened to Baby Jane*?

The relationship between Bette and her biological daughter was fairly complicated.

B.D. had claimed a loving childhood, but had some qualms about Bette's part in her adult life. Much of their grief may be traced to 1963, when Bette and B.D. were in Cannes to promote *What Ever Happened to Baby Jane*, which of course starred Davis but as earlier mentioned, also featured a teenaged B.D. in a small role. There, the young girl met Jeremy Hyman, who she would marry just a year later. She was 16 and he was twice her age.

Whatever the cause for the tome, *My Mother's Keeper* pained the actress greatly, and mother and daughter severed ties. Davis eventually took the time to finish her own bestselling autobiography, *This 'n That* (1987), part of which was written while she recovered from a stroke. Though the book detailed her battle with illness, it also contained an open letter addressed to her daughter, including the lines, "*I've been your keeper all these many years…,*" a clever hit, of course, on the title of B.D.'s controversial book.

This 'n That was actually Bette Davis' second biography. She had previously penned *A Lonely Life* in 1962. In it, she mentioned how human relationships were not dependable, and that it was in work where one could find true satisfaction. She would affirm that statement later, describing work as "*the least disappointing relationship*" one could have. In her history, save perhaps for her son, Michael (who defended her and later established a foundation in her name), many of her relationships did indeed end up disappointing her. But her work – her work was as enriching for her as it was for the world of entertainment.

Legacy: Larger Than Life

Bette Davis had a very singular approach to her craft. To be natural, she said, was not the point of acting and so she never bothered with being low-key. Acting, she is reported as saying, *"should be larger than life."* But it wasn't only her performances that were massive; she herself loomed large over everyone else. She harbored no illusions or pretensions that she was anything other than an outsize personality. She was aware of her talents and what these talents entitled her to, but she also imbued her gifts with a sense of responsibility. Of her reputation as being exacting and difficult at work, she had once said that she had to have a care for her output because *"It's your name up there."*

Providing quality work was also about accountability.

She was fearless and relentless, a true trailblazer who was aware of her own worth, and made sure everyone else knew about it too. In one endearing story, part of the Kennedy Center Honors' practice was to send out letters to people distinguished in their fields, asking them for suggestions on honorees for the year. In the early 1980s, Bette sent her suggestion to Washington: "*Me.*"

A few years later, the 79-year-old would indeed be honored by the Kennedy Center in 1987, in a ceremony at the White House of President Ronald Reagan – whom she had actually starred with in *Dark Victory*.

She played it cool of course, but it must have been gratifying to thus be honored by an industry she had paid so much to continue to be a part of. Bette Davis loved awards and didn't take the accolades sent her way for granted. Of her Oscars, she once said she was never "*a bit modest about them.*" She had also been quoted as admitting to a sense of 'greediness' about them, in that though she had "*gotten just about every award there is,*" she just "*can't have too many.*"

Bette Davis was prone to hyperbole, but when she mentioned getting pretty much all the awards out there, she wasn't too far off the mark. Aside from Oscars, an Emmy, and the Kennedy Center honor earlier mentioned, she was given the American Film Institute's Life Achievement Award in 1977 – the first woman to receive the distinction.

Much of her later awards were, appropriately, not just about individual film work anymore, but the body of her contributions. In 1989, she was also celebrated at the yearly Tribute of the Film Society of Lincoln Center. There were 2,700 people in the audience, and they gave her an almost 2-minute standing ovation. Her response? An iconic line from *Beyond the Forest* (1949): *"What a dump!"*

What a legend.

In 1980, she was also awarded the Defense Department's Distinguished Civilian Service Medal, for her work with the Hollywood Canteen during World War II. Here, she found a way to merge her dedication to her craft with her patriotism. When the United States went to war after the attack on Pearl

Harbor, thousands of Hollywood on and off-screen players responded to the call to serve. Davis couldn't fight in the field, but she did what she could at home by helping to establish and run a club catering to uniformed American recruits and Allies. She, along with actor John Garfield and businessman Jules Stein, were the force behind The Hollywood Canteen. It was a refuge of food and entertainment for uniformed men. Thousands of Hollywood workers – including actors and actresses! – volunteered at the Canteen to serve those who served the country. On some evenings, men about to go on dangerous tours even got to dance with a celebrity. There were lesser starlets helping out of course, but if the tales are accurate, Marlene Dietrich and Hedy Lamarr had washed dishes here. Rita

Hayworth served food. Betty Grable was there to welcome the millionth guest to walk in too – with a kiss. The project was a big success, and inspired the movie, *Hollywood Canteen* (1944). Over the years that it was open, estimates are that it welcomed 3 million servicemen to its doors.

These achievements are lofty and she had every right to be proud of them, for they cost her a lot too. She had paid for her achievements with a mostly lonely personal life, as well as exhausting effort as her health declined.

In 1983, she was diagnosed with breast cancer and needed a mastectomy. Shortly afterwards, she suffered a stroke. Months later, she had to have surgery for a broken hip. Her hurts would have a dire impact on her appearance and mobility, but she moved onwards as she does, always onwards with working. Through the difficulties of illness and old age, she fought on and continued to appear on film and television. She even continued to work after her daughter B.D.'s scathing book came out.

Through the vicissitudes of life she always had her beloved work and the industry was lucky to still have her, but by the late-1980s, they – *we* - wouldn't have her for very long anymore.

Her last major part was in *The Whales of August* (1987), where she played Libby Strong, a cantankerous, blind widow staying in her family's summer cottage with her sister, played by fellow Hollywood gem, Lillian Gish. They both gave powerhouse performances in roles that were a gift to accomplished actresses at the twilight of their years and careers.

Her last actual film, however, was *Wicked Stepmother* (1989), which she left mid-production; the first she would abandon thus in her career. She was initially said to have left for health reasons. She needed extensive dental work and suffered severe weight loss from its effects. But eventually, Bette Davis aired out her grievances against the director's style and wanted to distance herself from the project. It was rewritten and the final cut still included her, and so though the world was gifted with a final Bette Davis movie, it wasn't her best one.

Not that anything could have been so horrible as to dent her legacy at that point of her life. More than a slander on her work ethic, her exit from *Wicked Stepmother* showed she was, at 81, ailing but apparently still feisty. But she had also suffered a series of strokes, and her cancer would return. When the doctors informed her the cancer had spread and her situation was terminal, she was told to just go on about her life.

In Bette's case, "life" was work and so, work she did.

In 1989, she was dying of cancer, in pain and had impaired mobility. But there was an award with her name on it at a film festival in San Sebastian, Spain, and so she had to get it. From Los Angeles she headed off to Europe, but she wouldn't make it back home alive.

In the French leg of her return to the United States, she became too weak and needed to be hospitalized. She died a few days later, on the 6th of October. Shortly before she died, she was still busy updating her 1962 autobiography, *The Lonely Life*, and catching it up with what transpired in her life since it first came out.

All-too-fittingly, just as she closed her life with that award in Spain, the last of the five new chapters she prepared for the book was written in San Sebastian. The last chapter in her life, and the last chapter of her book… It's almost, well, cinematic.

No one could have written her own life out better than Bette.

Printed in Great Britain
by Amazon